SOME OTHER SKY

This book is dedicated to the memory of my late parents, Glenn and Sheila Mary Fahner, and to my grandmother, Alice Ennis, who was so very dear to me. It is also dedicated to the memory of my friend, Tom Ryan, whom I miss dearly, and who was always so supportive of my creative work; and to my sister, Stacy.

Previously published works

"Leavetaking" was published in The Lake (Winter 2013)
"He would give it to me" was published in Grain (Volume 42.2, Winter 2014)
"St. Luke's Lovers" and "Dearest," were published in Sulphur (2013)
"Good Company" was published in The Human Journal (2013)
"Looking for Light" and "Woman of the Birches" were published in Open Minds Quarterly (August 2016)
"Little Cree Women (Sisters, Secrets & Stories) was published in Writers Against Prejudice (Summer 2016)
"Traveling the Fish, Stornoway" was published in Ofi Press Magazine (Winter 2016)
"Field Notes from a Northern Mining Town" was published in The Interpreter's House, Issue 66, October 2017

Some Other Sky

Kim Fahner

Black Moss Press
2017

Library and Archives Canada Cataloguing in Publication

Fahner, Kim, 1970-, author
    Some other sky / Kim Fahner.

Poems.
ISBN 978-0-88753-582-6 (softcover)

    I. Title.

PS8561.A3784S66 2017   C811'.54   C2017-903348-4

Cover image: Trish Stenabaugh, Untitled, 2010, acrylic on canvas
Author photo: Gerry Kingsley
Design: Karen Veryle Monck

 Black Moss
EST. 1969 Press   Published by Black Moss Press
2450 Byng Road
Windsor, ON N8W 3E8 Canada
www.blackmosspress.com

Black Moss books are distributed in Canada and the U.S. by Fitzhenry & Whiteside. All orders should be directed there.

Black Moss Press acknowledges the support of the Canada Council for the Arts and the Ontario Arts Council for its publishing program.

 ONTARIO ARTS COUNCIL
CONSEIL DES ARTS DE L'ONTARIO

 Canada Council   Conseil des Arts
for the Arts   du Canada

PRINTED IN CANADA

Contents

This City

Mine since birth, this city,
nickel labyrinth under foot,
made by meteor, sent by stars,
built on ancient bones;
time before time,
sweet grass and pine,
birch and blue water.

Rock outcrops thumbprint
what lies beneath, mark
what came before
and still exists.

In deepest winter,
robin's egg sky
calls to me, so that
boots crunch on new snow,
cedar scents crisp air,
and dogs rustle up the road.

Out into woods now,
chorus of chickadees,
black crows spread wings wide,
guard land, soar high above,
while red foxes and rabbits
carve pathways where
humans cannot go.

Mine since the beginning, this city,
weaves a dreamcatcher,
echoes of ancestors,
reminders of the past
before moving forward.

Inherited, this city,
family full of its stories,
tales yet to be told,
edging along its coppered cliff,
out towards beyond,
where Creighton once stood,
now ghosted and made pale.

Ours since origin, this city,
reforested rock and interior lakes;
its people, our people,
its heart, our hearts,
dreams of future built on past,
shatter cones and fault lines
like bones under earth.

Still, look up, raise your eyes to sky,
see promise of evolution,
wrapped in birch bark and
carried on the breath
of this shared dream.

St. Luke's Lovers

On the night I saw
spring's first geese
string themselves across
a pre-dusk sky,
two lovers sat, solitary,
on the front step of a church.

Huddled close,
sharing a smoke,
they seemed united
against the world,
guarded by God—
their incense rising
to sky and universe.

Homeward then,
and there are feathers,
four or more,
left precisely on pavement,
so that I wonder if
some fallen angels
will guide me home.

Dearest,

I have sautéed the zucchini,
plated it with care,
so that it waits for you,
as do I,
with semblance of patience,
but underlying frisson of urgency.

For the rain has frozen,
the roads are slick,
and time ticks onward,
while I wait
in winter.

Respite

Driving back into town,
speeding over worn asphalt,
the mine's head frame rises over rock,
rooting deep into earth, into memory;
this place is black basin born,
made of meteor.

The sky is pale tangerine in early July,
lake water deepest blue, rippled,
trees feather green, watercolours,
so that I forget pain of winter—
snow banks six feet deep,
cutting out paths for dogs & car,
the growl and scrape of plows at 5am,
the frostbite that eats at feet
through thick boots,
relentless in its pursuit.

Along Elgin,
freight trains crawl
past station and market,
rails cutting through heart of town,
stopping cars on Elm Street;
people are made to wait, sit, think.

Respite now from the elements
speaks to me of days spent
planting solar lanterns, pansies,
day lilies and daisies, fingers
deep into potting soil, loam
licking under fingernails and
then wedging there with certainty.

Quick. Before November comes,
take a deep breath, hold it,
until winter passes once again,
until I can be free to cast off
heavy coats and not wear socks.

Field Notes from a Northern Mining Town

Gordon Pinsent haunts me,
emerging from behind
trunks of shrunken autumn trees,
slinking along city sidewalks,
even waiting for a night bus
scheduled never to arrive.

He would like it here,
his Newfoundland rock
finding its mate in drifts
of buried nickel ore:

I imagine him walking,
weather worn and salty,
on some cinematic screen,
down Elgin, passing flat irons,
darkened streets and
shadow women.

Past the woman who
sits solitary, paints
her face with colour,
and entertains drivers—
blowing up condoms and
then letting them go,
like spent balloons.

Despair still lives here,
leaning up against the market wall,
darkened stage silhouettes,
the chaos of a man lying on a park bench,
but symmetry in the way
his shoes sit—perfectly paired—
underneath the wooden bench,
waiting for morning.

Woman of the Birches

Swaying in wind, trees speak
in whispers, testing her
as she tries to decipher meaning
from this northern ground.

Translation isn't easy;
here, rock rising sharply from snow,
she struggles to find her footing,
grasps onto the bough of nearby pine or sumac
so that snow clumps and falls.

Not graceful, walking in woods,
but still grace somehow arrives;
she unearths secrets and
remembers ghosts of herself
from her youth.

Woman of the birches stands still,
raises her arms up in semblance of quiet victory,
directing woodland symphony while still
trying to discern peace inside.

Peeling back layers,
birch bark like skin,
she searches and
never seems to find.

Bury Something

(inspired by Glen Hansard)

In every generation,
someone buries something,
whether they want to or not:
a worn valise, a lost baby,
a memory of love, or a secret.

Sometimes you need to bury something
to let go of what's past,
to usher in bright newness
and start all over again.

No one said it would be easy;
there were never any guarantees.
You just assumed things
couldn't get any worse.

You were wrong.

Before things blossom,
they often lie fallow,
left for dead in raised flower beds
over empty winter months,
waiting for spring to rise again.

The same is true of you,
who thinks the world is over,
who cannot fathom tomorrow,
but will live to see the sun
rise once more.

Looking for Light

In winter here,
sky melds with snowy land,
so sun shadows play tricks
on your eyes, transforming
clouds into high snow drift.

I'm out here, alone,
looking for light
and finding it where
least expected:

in rabbit tracks up a wooded hill,
in the sound of dogs scuffling,
in the weave of cedars
that silhouette themselves
against this February air.

Kaleidoscope

The inside of her head
reverberates, voices spinning
round in kaleidoscope fashion.

Is this what a Picasso painting
feels like, turned inside out,
all sharp edges and angles?
Or, is it all mirrors, fragments
and shards, slicing and sawing?
Tiring. Knots tied, untied,
and then tied again. Attempts
to gather things together, futile.

Nothing here is recognizable.

Delusions spin through space,
hallucinations babble,
bubble, hands move without
sense of purpose or intent,
plain sight distorted by
shadowed figures dressed
in paranoia and suspicion.

There are no longer any
nuanced voices, no clear pathways,
no anchors upon which
she can depend.

One voice says *ugly, fat, boring*,
while another questions her clothes or hair;
they watch, overhear, spy,
fashion darkened delusion.

Head spins, outward, inward,
slash, mind sliced open
so that thinking spills out,
unwieldy, frazzled, distorted,
and now spent.

Bird Cage

The ripple startles,
sharp slice between breasts,
emerges from inside curve of ribs,
from within that skeletal cage,
so that heart feels like it is breaking—
twinges, snaps, stretches outwards
and then releases and flutters,
like a wounded bird.

These are wings, sprouting,
feathers creating space inside body,
beating harder than heart
and then threatening
to begin only by destroying.

This bird struggles within its bony cage,
pulls relentlessly at muscles, pokes at lungs,
until it is hard to find stillness inside.

Open up:
take deep breaths,
let go of the edge,
trust that leap will conjure flight.
Push off and up, against despair,
kick hard, release, rise.

Thirst

The house sips slowly
at the offerings of
bowls that sit, solitary,
on ancient radiators.

It devours silently,
savouring water
that lowers itself slowly,
reduces itself, erases,
until painted bowls
remain, naked,
with only skin of water
leaving a full moon
on bottom of
concave ceramic.

I fill and then re-fill,
wondering which ghosts
drink at night, what echoes
of memory might dance
through shadows, round
painted corners and through
the French doors.

The house sips, slowly,
reminds me that all things
vanish, with time, with patience.

Thunder in Lumsden

Birds circle, feathers
sweeping shingles,
frantic as they hear
the beginnings of
a far off rumble,
finely tuned
to catastrophe.

The sky here clouds
over itself, pulls atmosphere
down and around buildings,
and then the rain begins,
bouncing off the pavement
outside the window,
swallowing up a distant hill
and clutch of pines,
all before it sweeps land,
shifts left to right,
herds birds and then
shuffles prairie dogs.

Birds spin, frenzied,
darting.

Inside, stillness.

Little Cree Women (Sisters, Secrets & Stories)

(after an art exhibit by Brittney & Richelle Bear Hat)

Middle of northern Alberta bush:
shadows flickering over rough ground,
as a lover would trace the quiet arc of shoulder
or neglected curve of bent knee.

One big pine, solitary and strong,
framing a suggestion of camp fire—
wood smoking, kindling cracking.
Kokum said, "*If you gossip about bears,
you will call one in.*" And so he came,
like a truth you can't avoid,
paws padding and breath snuffling,
before the hour was out.

Then, nudging us to find other parts
of ourselves there, like beads
worked perfectly into the likeness
of a blushing Arctic rose
fastened firmly to deer hide—
soft moccasins to wear
with each new step forward.

And then,
long braids of sweet grass and
tightly woven offerings of
sacred sage and tobacco, for smudging.
Willow bark and charred wood,
nested in a wreath of
white flowers and mint leaves.

These woods, filled with sun and wind,
water and stars, gather us in,
remind us of who we are
long after others have forgotten
and the fox still dreams,
restless in shifting leaf shadows.

Truth Telling

(for Beverley McLachlin, the Chief Justice of Canada)

Nokomis nudges Owl, gesturing
so that Owl finds her courage, speaks:
"Come and enter the circle."

She invites me four times,
haunting calls from near
the wide water's side,
while Cormorant sails high
next to Eagle's wings—
passing dragonflies
and monarchs.

"Come and enter the circle;
sit in this living tree—
gather up your broken hearts,
red dresses and unfinished moccasins.
Find the oldest, most forbidden words.
Find the stories and tell them now.
You are right here with us."

Owl tucks her head under her wing,
nestled up to sleep, when Nokomis
nudges her again, urges her to speak:
"Come and enter the circle.
We are all here to stay."

And so I go, tread gently,
reach out an open palm to Owl,
nod to the birds and insects,
bow to the trees and ferns,
let them lead me into the circle, ask:
"But why do you let me in?"

Nokomis smiles, vast skies
crossing the blue of her eyes,
clouds passing and tears falling,
and she speaks while Owl listens:
"You are right here with us.
We are all here to stay.
Now, we begin again, reconciling."

And Owl's wings open wide—
a swirl of feathered regalia,
a shawl surrounding a dancer,
a sacred drum sounding
an ancient heartbeat.

This is a bright beadwork story told
from the far reaches of Vancouver Island
eastward to Pincher Creek, further still
to the edges of Lake Erie's Pelee.
On from the rushing water
of the Ottawa River,
and to Manitoulin's shores—
and then, further still,
north to Attawapiskat.

They gather me in, these wide wings,
invite me to enter the circle,
leave me bending down to earth,
picking up beads cast off in the past—
gathering them to begin again,
to fasten them onto deer hide
with needle and thread,
so flowers blossom once more,
nestled together and moving forward.

Fearless

He lifts his small arms high to sky,
calling out with unbridled voice,
reaching up as if wanting to fly,
shouting with joy that rises above
the crashing thunder of Pacific surf.

She stands five feet behind,
letting him take in the sun, water,
world, willing him to enter into
whatever life will bring.

Watching, from here,
further down the shore,
sensing silver threads
trailing from one to the other;
braided, not divided.

He squeals, delighted,
calling to the universe,
wings unbound from between
scrawny shoulder blades,
feathers stretching out,
reaching, spanning sky,
until he lifts, soul
above small body,
leaving fear behind—
a puddle of dried seaweed,
ribboned and curled.

Meditation on Ucluelet

Bend to touch long fingers
to the surface of pressed sand, skin grazing;
push palm into the certainty of sea floor
sometime before tide returns,
sweeping with it mermaid scales
and tumbled blue-green sea glass.

Step forward, boldly, toes bared
to late March sun;
bend again now, dipping your hand
into pale foam of new waves landing,
licking at feet. Retreat, advance,
and then once more, until a small step
taken hesitantly towards shore
feels more damning than free,
until an eagle soars high above
and offers its wings in sacred flight.

Touch palm to lips.

Taste salt water—
tongue awake now, words spilling out,
rushed lines falling to earth through air,
until stanzas write themselves in cursive
on this once hidden ocean floor,
now revealed in brightest light.

And so, sing a pacific song,
trailing ribbons of seaweed
in the hope that someone finds
this path of broken shells—
painted mothered pearl and turquoise;
in the belief that someone follows,
as waves always return
to their place of origin,
under moon's nudging
sun's watchful gaze.

Fish Point, Pelee Island

Round, shore pebbles
sit in my palm, cupped.

They are as I wish you were—
weighted, substantial, and then
clearly defined by curved borders.

Bird song in the trees above;
voices of birders murmur below,
softly, binoculars poised—
a checklist to be marked,
one bright orange oriole,
and the other,
a red-winged blackbird.

My fingers are deep in sand,
sifting and searching
for sea glass and shells,
all mothered pearl and milky mist.

Hands holding worn stones,
some tiny as lost punctuation marks,
some like pebbled ovals—
best for skipping—
worried by lake waters,
tumbled by endless rounds
of catch and release.

Standing, I feel my knees
begin to creak, and my
heart start to fray at the edges—
fingers searching for meaning
and pulling at stray threads
of memory and love.

It deepens into love

Geese sweep across this morning's sky,
moving separately, but woven
together in tight formation—
feathers arc, wings raise
and then lower.

Waves lap against this pebbled shore,
consistent and certain,
a seaworthy sense of ebb and flow—
returning, again and again,
persistent, to meet the steadfast
shelf of limestone, eroding so
slowly, sculpting time.

This ache, this broken heart
you left behind,   ·
strips me from stem to stern,
adrift, dogpaddling for shore.

And they say, with time,
the ache will pass,
deaden itself and shift,
until it deepens
into love, until I find
pieces of you, fossils,
in the sand at my feet.

A Curtailed Glosa: Phoenix Rising

But his poems come back
like sudden rain in a desert, one recited line
flowering into the next,
a small recovered miracle.
> —Alice Major, "Eve waters the garden"

Days like peony petals—
painted ribbons, scissor-curled and twisted,
segments of self, wrapped like presents;
clementines waiting to be opened, slowly,
seductively, with conviction. At the sun's rising,
even the trees weave, shiver, and crack,
waiting for metaphor to speak, mouth words,
promise light. Press up against darkness &
fight this night's deepest black,
but still *his poems come back.*

Words etched in nightblindness,
fluorescent scrolling mapped out in stars,
so that constellations crisscross hearts,
conjure up memory and loss. Raspberry
blushes on pale skin, erasure, and then
a rising. Phoenix-feathered, soaring up to pines,
rejuvenate, reanimate, reclaim and lift above.
Search out sustenance, longing for words,
syllables and rhymes, vivid images, white wine—
like sudden rain in a desert, one recited line.

Don't gift me with a spare sonnet;
I can't begin to decipher those tight rhymes,
but spend time longing for free verse—
searching for patterns in a William Morris design.
Meaning woven through stanzas, words
thought, spoken, and even misplaced text.
My heart a faded weather balloon, spent;
my mind like brightened lavender-mint tea,
one moment steeping, then perplexed,
somehow *flowering into the next.*

Walking under the tall chinquapin oaks,
lovers in each other's arms,
a Great Blue Heron stands, statue.
Turned sideways to the world,
a feathered poem, wings stretched out,
all blue-grey, hollow bones and graceful eye.
This heart, wind-blown and open wide,
lost words and thoughts, mind mazed;
hope is a piece of green sea glass, a tremble,
a small recovered miracle.

A Week at Woodbridge Farm
(for Grant)

This house, like a ship,
looks out to the horizon;
it watches, takes a breath
and then exhales.

It hears the sound of
water meeting land,
as certain as a heartbeat—
steadfast as the pale shade
of a ghosted lighthouse
on a nearby Pelee shore.

Cormorants and gulls
catch themselves
on high wind currents,
while the ferry's horn
marks its passage through
white-capped waves.

In late afternoon,
the light changes,
so the house paints itself gold—
silhouettes of leaves
etched on high columns,
and sun deepens its yellow brick.

Outside, dragonflies dance
and monarchs glide, caught up
on breath of air—joyful.
Somewhere, an owl speaks,
and trees gather her in—
sheltered, safe now.

Soon, the house sees skies
painted at sunset, watches clouds shift,
making way for moon and stars;
it takes a breath in and then exhales,
in time with the pendulum
of a lakeside night swing.

The Kingsville Sequence

I)
A murmuration
rises up above long road
catches breath, breaks heart

II)
Thunder at sunrise
ripples electric
trees shiver and wake

III)
Night swing in Kingsville
shadow dogs snuffle
humid sky lowers

IV)
Where point stretches out,
birds gather, water swirls,
waves break open heart

V)
Searching out sea glass,
pale green or sky blue fragments,
sunset hovering

The Great Lakes Sequence

Memory Landscapes: A Photographic Lineage
(after Barry Ace)

And the memory of story
will speak itself into being,
shift voice from Crow to Owl to Eagle,
stretch out its wings and settle in—
never solid enough to capture again,
never trusting that words are enough
for what the heart knows.

It will serve as conjurer and magician,
this story-memory, clothed in deerskin
and gilded by late afternoon sun,
paddles lifted from float of water's surface,
so that it sits solitary, meditative, waiting.

From small puddles of mossy water
in depth of northern bush,
where bracken is more present than not;
from ponds, where woodland streams
curl themselves secretive through
last year's forgotten leaves;
from the quiet place that sits
between two branches, joined by
a rough path for hard portage;
from big water, where shorelines
disappear if you look away for too long,
or even—without thinking—dare to blink.

And the memory of the story
will give itself voice again,
telling of fish that have vanished,
only skeletons left behind,
erased by slow and steadfast progress,
something that seems like destruction
if you squint your eyes together
to look hard enough into the sun,
or something that you can resurrect
with hope, crossed fingers, and a spare prayer.

Turtle Island

Tall grasses near shore
bend graceful and move themselves,
willowed, all spirited
and standing as guardians.

Hidden there, a turtle,
its green-black mossy shell
fixed to a fallen log, certain,
next to another which suns itself.

This is a pair with no losses—
turtle within turtle,
mated one to the other—
beaded first on birch bark canvas,
and then tattooed on
heart's flesh and fibre,
so that you cannot forget that
this is where you are rooted.

On the Great Crosswaters Sea

(for Lake Huron; Gichi-aazhoogami-gichigami)

On the shores of this vast
Great Crosswaters Sea,
we scramble over Group of Seven
sculpted shorelines, holding hands
and breathless now,
looking out over water.

The sky sinks down
and seduces us so that
we sit, legs bared and
stretched out against granite,
pale skin blooming pink in the sun.

One hand against side of lighthouse,
holding me up; the other, raised to
shade eyes, looking out to far horizon.
There, down the channel, a fishing boat,
chugging along and belching gasoline,
while a radio crackles, broken, from the docks.

Beyond that spit of land,
across the water, somewhere,
the promise of Manitowaning sits,
a smaller sister of lighthouse
calling in fishermen, a one-eyed siren
overlooking the bay and the stretch
of land that curves over to Wikwemikong.

From Killarney to Manitoulin,
across Huron's bruised blue sea,
a boat once traveled, home-made
and much-loved, with blankets for sails,
rope pooled at the base of a mast, a pulley
raising and lowering with the steady rhythm
of lovers caught up in a night storm.

On the Chain of Lakes Sea

(for Lake Erie; Aanikegamaa-gichigami)

This love song for Erie
tugs at my heart,
strings plucked on a
neglected violin,
then sounded after
long silence.

A southwestern reaching,
a web on a map read in the north,
a geometry of heart that
speaks to "lines" and "concessions,"
cartography my father spoke
from the passenger seat
before he left, trailing wisdom
and story behind him.

Those fields, with roads that
divided and square-framed them
like old mottled Polaroids:

Memories of strawberry suppers
in long church basements near Exeter,
in July's deepest heat, our legs stuck to plastic chairs
in gingham shorts and feet swinging beneath us.

Graveyards, searching out lost ones,
trying to find the thread that linked
one to the other, finding self in stones,
names etched deep into farm's lands.

And then, as a grown up, down to Pelee Island,
out on an uncertain ferry that reminds me of Colville,
all white and blue, all ship and water,
all spaces through which I see things:

Scatters of stones, pebbled up on shores
strewn with leftover coal from shipwrecks,
ghosts grazing ground where sand meets water,
searching for sea glass to put in their pockets.

A house like a ship, perched on cusp of hill;
an owl that speaks softly in dawn's earliest stirring;
a stanza made up of yellow brick and dragonflies.

On the Anishinaabeg Sea

(for Lake Superior, Anishinaabewi-gichigami,
& for my grandmother, Alice)

When she died,
the pebbles she had gathered
from each Great Lake's shore
stood in a small round rose bowl—
clear glass and pregnant—
on the kitchen windowsill.

On road trips,
she sat in the back seat,
between us, gazing out car windows
with longing in her eyes—
searching out a stone shore
and then asking to stop,
sensing a skim of blue water
off to the left of asphalt divided
by yellow lines and hemmed in
by guard rails that folded into themselves,
and gleamed bright silver in sun.

Green station wagons
in the early 80s
found their way onto
graveled shoulders of roads
that curled into forests
where broad leaf and pine trees
mingled without chaperones,
getting up to no good.

Every place had a pebble,
offered her a touchstone,
and every town sent a postcard,
her hand cursive and full of love.

When she died, the stones still sat
on the kitchen windowsill,
but no one covered them with water
so they faded, lost their spirit,
longed for their past places and spaces,
wondered where the woman had gone—
she who had held pebbles in the curve of her palm,
fingers tracing arcs and worrying them
like rosary beads on a dark night.

On the Illinois Sea

(for Lake Michigan, Ininwewi-gichigami, & for my father, Glenn)

This Hudson Bay blanket
makes me think of the one
that splayed itself colonial
in my great-grandfather's house,
to be used at the foot of a bed, decoratively,
or to cover cold knees on a winter night,
all utilitarian and minimal.

Splice your colours, divide and conquer,
parse this soul from that one,
count the feet in each line of poetry,
try to figure out the equation
of a life well lived.

Crossing the long bridge
while using emergency speeds,
passing Mackinac Island
in the dead of night,
car's headlights in the rearview mirror
behind me; you, flown ahead and
landing in Petoskey.

Petoskey: a name I'd never heard before;
a father lying broken in a bed;
a hospital on the edge of a lake;
a sunrise after no sleep and
endless cups of machine-made coffee;
a place wandered at the end of day,
sucking in fresh air after hours of
'what if' and 'what comes next' and
'how can I fix this?'

Michigan: the place you go to
when your own won't take you;
the people who gather you in,
the lake that brings your heart peace
when nothing else offers it.

On the Big Lake

(for Lake Ontario, Gichi-zaagaʼigan)

*"Our first teaching on water begins in our mother's womb.
This land is not for sale, or profit. We need to come together for water."*
——Autumn Peltier

The words are passed, one to another,
mother to daughter, aunty to niece,
a sacred Ojibway language that tells
a string of stories that say
water is the blood of Mother Earth.

All great water passes through
this vast lake of shining waters;
it travels across farmers' fields,
seeps into earth and feeds crops,
ties itself to the St. Lawrence,
umbilical curls and memories of
ancestors who must shiver at
the possibility of pipelines
and clear cuts of tall pines.

She is a water walker,
someone who tells me, knowingly,
Everything is water. Everything.
This pond, this river, this still frozen lake—
all keepers of memory.

From the fish that swim deepest waters,
to the birds that dip down to drink,
to the humans who settle on its
industrialized shorelines, this lake
is provincial, stretching out from
west to east, a waterway to travel on,
a journey to be taken with heart open wide.

Looking Down, 1988

(for Alex Colville)

Here is what lies submerged beneath:
a battered heart, hitched up breath, a sigh,
an exhale that speaks of wanting to dive downwards,
again, to find what's been lost or forgotten;
a flash of fish-silvered fins, quick now,
summer sun in water reflected.

The essence of a man, Tilley-clad, all white,
and a woman, drifting a hand down to water,
palm skimming and rippling blue—
quick now, before the winds pick up
and the clouds cover sky in mirrored sea.

Horse and Train, 1954

(for Alex Colville)

Searched for this one,
waited with bated breath,
having only seen it once
or twice as a child,
Colville seduced, image of
single dark horse racing
towards fast speeding train.

Always thought,
somehow,
the horse would win,
even though up against
such force and strength.

Now, having found it,
tucked into obscure corner of exhibit,
the sharp bright of headlight
silvers rails with implied endings.

Even though I want
that horse to win,
to triumph, dark mane flying,
hooves alive, eyes sharp with
promise, I know it will
likely lose, either swallowed up
by engine or sliding down
rail bed, clouds crowning it
as it goes.

Vignette

Solitary bicycle
leans up against bleached wall;
seems weary, bereft even.

Two doors down,
in a weathered blue house,
a dog sits in an upstairs window,
peering out, solemn white face
framed by worn yellow sill.

Up against Causkey's pub wall,
the sound of glasses clinking,
pints sloshing and voices,
slips out the front door, sliding into
narrow, twisted streets.

The Pink House,
named too obviously,
sits solitary, cracks ripping
façade so that tuft of green grass
grows outward into air, shifting
when the wind blows,
breezing itself towards ocean.

Further, off the lane that
leads down to the strand,
a scarecrow in yellow
rain slicker stands,
surveying field
and watching over
a clutch of rogue cows.

There should be a lighthouse,
but instead a sailboat sits
affixed to rock,
abandoned & forgotten,
in a place where the past
pulls itself forward
to live in the present.

Solitary Ceili

(after Anne Ffrench's video Until the End)

A whirl of bare feet
circle round, faster now,
until muslin and lace of skirt kicks up,
reveals ankles and then knees,
slip jig or mad reel,
spun like the song of a sparkled soul,
kaleidoscope crazy, solitary ceili,
a whirl of a girl searching for peace
in abandoned rooms.
A strange bird watches, perched on
a bed that has denied its own longings,
next to a chair that has
forgotten itself in decay,
and still the bird watches,
now careful, persistent, witness to
soul dancing in fractured light,
defiant, joyous, alive.

Good Company

(after Nicola Slattery)

This boat is worn, has carried many,
but now carries only a girl and her sheep
in true ark-like fashion.

The sea storms, all blue-green and white caps,
waves mounting and then crashing
against some unseen shore.

The moon, suspended in sky, sleeps soundly.
(It simply cannot worry itself with futile
human endeavours on Irish seas.)

Blue dress with red collar, she peers at sheep,
cradling its head in her hands, comforting it.
The sheep, ignoring her, peers out at the world,
with simple mind but knowing eyes.

On a Castletownbeare hill,
in someone's back garden,
an abandoned fishing boat,
clearly marked *The Mary Rose,*
leans sideways, achingly, towards sea—
as if it knows there will be no reunion.

Your ship has long since sailed away from me.
Same continent, different countries,
but I wonder, when the moon rises
and the sea shifts without us even knowing,
if you will ever miss me as much as I do you.

Love Song for Beara

And it was there, in Eyeries,
that I found myself, as a slow boat
puttered out into Coulagh Bay,
trailing silver in its wake.

Here, in this place where the Skelligs sit offshore,
cows dance, ducks quack, faeries scuttle, the dog speaks,
and the Ring of Kerry rises, but never bows down.

Paths swivel and surprise,
birds natter and gather,
ivy tangles trees, rooting itself in moss.

Sky moves, landscape shifts,
transforms itself with beams of sun—
paints green gold, warms & brightens day.

Taste ripe blackberries in the lanes, next to fields owned by coal black cows.
Buy cheap wine in the village to go with stew and stanzas.
Traipse through bog near strand and wonder if you will be found
the next day, after having fallen in.

Church bells, at noon and six, peal out to mark divisions of day.
Houses painted the colour of crayons, never to be erased.
Eight miles to Kilcatherine, over loping hills and curled lanes,
a two hour walk from there to here, from ancient graveyard
to seaside pub with picture window and pints.

Out of darkness, out of past lives,
of love and lost love,
of life and lost life,
memory bound, this place,
etched on heart.

A Byzantine Promise

(for W.B. Yeats)

In a Drumcliffe churchyard,
I gather stones in the palm
of my hand, run fingers along
smooth curves and arcs,
sense syllables and ghosts
of leftover words, trace
the letters of his name
on my bruised heart.

Down Sligo's rainy streets,
he strides:
here, a stanza that falls
forgotten from a spare pocket,
there, a heart broken by
the women not
brave enough
to love him.

I carry his poems close,
so that he walks with me,
through veils and then back again,
weaving through a world
full of weeping.

If I had known you, I whisper,
touching Benbulben's feet again,
I would have held you in my arms,
listened to your mad dreamings,
written you sonnets of seduction,
crossed my heart with a Byzantine
promise, given you strong anchor
in a frantic and too stormy sea.

But the words on his stone
tell me to pass by, to not tread
on his dreams, to walk my own path,
gather heart breaks like the simple
marsh daisies that grow down by the sea,
stringing them into a chain of memory.

Leavetaking

(for Seamus Heaney)

This afternoon,
in a beam of late summer light,
a sweep of starlings rose up
from the maple on the corner.

Here, far across an ocean,
the leaves ripple and turn over,
the birds' feathers stir, so that,
it seems, even the air currents
carry news of your going.

Your words conjure
western roads overlooking
a windy sea, resurrect
bog bodies, recall borders
made by men and not land.

On night walks,
crisp in fall, dogs at my feet,
I search through stars,
as though for miracles and postscripts,
even as I root down through
earth beneath me, a Sagittarian, torn.

Along Moniack's Verges

In the field next door,
a spare black cow stretches out
into the shape of an early morning
sun salutation, pressing upward from earth,
hooves blackened with rain, sharp against green;
shape shifting from downward facing dog
into the certainty of tadasana
without the benefit of toes.

That road, with its passing spaces
clearly labelled, offers the sound
of a bird *tick, tick, ticking*
amidst the low branches of pine
draped in blue-green lichen—
a veil through which stonechats flit.

Gather up sprigs of gorse. Snap tall purpled grasses,
oxeye daisies, bog myrtle, and primrose
with quick fingers, for pressing
between pages. Memories to take
back across such a vast sea—
juniper and heather carried over salt water,
images imprinted on the heart.

The sky is swept clean by busy clouds—
wind through defiant curls,
footsteps solitary on worn pavement.
Sound of rubber soles on road swallowed up
by the aura of carved Caledonian hills, pine clad.

Syllables of sound drift:
hawk in flight, wings always beating,
all rush of air and power;
dogs rushing to the neighbour's fence,
excitement in flip of tail and loll of tongue;
hearing wind through branches,
feeling green dreaming of ancient roots.

Each bend fastens itself firmly in my mind,
the sky's light shivering and transforming hills
into the deep silver of a mid-July night.
The road travelled down
is not the road you return upon.

Cursive Courting

Martin says, over supper one night,
 a glass full of red wine in his hand:
"A man can fall in love to handwriting, you know."

The upwards reach of the *r*, rooted and certain,
carrying on from base to rise of an implied hillside.
And then the swoop of a wide *w*, reminds of curves,
a hand around a waist, fingers tracing neck's slope,
a spin at a dance, a bird in air, the shape of lips kissing.

The sense of a sea journey in an *s*, carved cursive
into the shape of a ship's sail, a journey over salt water
and then an arrival, strong feet rooted to land's edge,
beginning again after an ending. A finger tracing
patterns in spilled salt on a worn kitchen table.

The intimacy of a *z*, a 'zed' and not a 'zee,'
two curled into one another, looped yet still distinct,
and then the kiss of a *k*, wound and entwined,
a bit of coloured yarn fashioned into a wobbly form.
Not to forget the strength of a *t*, arms out, open,
the promise of embraces, fastened with the
perfect closure of an *o*, someone who amazes,
jaw-dropping surprise, never ending.
A button sewn on tight, not to be lost.

And so Martin says, again,
"A man can, you know.
Fall in love to a woman's handwriting.
I know it. I have done."

The women listening sigh,
take their breaths back, and
think of the potential of fresh ink
etched out, silhouette on a blank page.

You'll Be Needing to Write a Love Letter (to a Man Who Can Grate Carrots)

Deborah passes me the recipe,
all Baskerville and laminated,
saying that grating is what's required
for this Scottish salad.

"At home, in Canada," I say,
"I only chop. I don't grate."

She smiles, shakes her head,
offers me the stainless steel
pyramid, hole-riddled, finger-hungry,
and then replies, cheekily:
"Then you'd best find a man
who can grate carrots, eh?"

To Find You

And I will walk,
over high hills and
near cusps of basalt-blackened cliffs,
so weathered by sea spray,
and through the low heather waiting
to bloom in August,
amidst sharp thistles,
to find you.

I will come, then,
on the wings of high white birds,
dipping feathers above long twists
of switch-backed roads and
endless lengths of those
tumbled stone walls
that lace themselves,
seductively, through fields.

And so, I will wait,
as the sea waits for her men to return
after a summer's fierce storm,
and as the mountain holds its breath
for this wild sky's touch, tendrils of
mist reaching down, so tentative
and nearly trembling now.

And I will offer ribbons made of raw silk
to the branches of rowan trees,
bending low to feel bark on my back,
and longing for your hands on the
slope of my shoulders.

And so, I will wait for you,
the sun tracing triskeles
on my fair skin, knotting
me with hopeful impatience.

What Do Birds Say?

Standing circle,
one next to the other,
tails painted and wings serrated,
these birds sing a dawn chorus,
highland bound:

Bright eyes, come here!

    Hello!
        I'm safe!

Come over here, darling!
    I'm over here, here, here.

Each other. Together.

    Praise, praise, anyway.

Darling, where are you?
    I'm over here, here, here.

Bright eyes, come here!

Each other. Together.

    Dance with me.
        Dance!

    Sing with me.
        Sing!

Spin
    circle
        dip wings, feathers,
on air currents,
        come around again.

Darling, where are you?
    I'm over here, here here.
    (Can't you find me?)

Storm at Stornoway

In that brief dark of northern night,
when the fine mist of rain shifted,
slicing into the sea without apology,
the lighthouse could not stop itself
from blinking its steady eye, the gulls
sent themselves into a frenzy, shattering
the pre-dawn quiet of a silvered harbour.

Wings beat against rain,
feathers angled and cutting
through grey of wettest air,
their calls like fishwives;
feathers and hollow bones
spinning ceilidh in circles,
spirals that edge on the too deep
ripple of thunder, catching up
heart in tempest, turned.

Traveling the Fish, Stornoway

She went to the fish,
following it around Lewis,
from outport to outport,
apron at the ready and
fingers wrapped up in clean rags
that ribboned themselves
around her once fine hands—
already stinging, sharp salted,
too pickled in that barrel brine.

She was Hebridean born,
strong enough to stand, to wait
in an empty yard, until the boats
came in from that cold sea,
chugging, shedding fish scales
and trailing dolphins in their wake,
bringing her twelve hours of work,
back breaking and sea gull attended,
so that feathers drifted from sky
to shore, landing at her feet.

Silver darlings, they were,
all fish bellies tight and full of guts,
until the knife sliced, until the woman
turned insides out, packed in salt
and made for far Europe.

Swift twist and turn of wrist,
she sang in Gaelic, the words
drifting across the pier, her hands
cut up and aching; the Selkies, hidden
just behind a harbour rock, watching.

Bringing Home the Peat, Isle of Lewis

The knot of heavy wool is pushed deep
into the space of her skirt pockets,
its threads laced through tired fingers,
even as she walks the paths of
Gearrannan, stones nestled lopsided
in the worn moss, green now at her feet.

Such a heavy weight, but she does not complain;
this keshie, a woven basket full of peat blocks,
piled high and bending her, nearly broken now,
like a weighted birch tree in a mid-October windstorm,
rain lashing and threatening to turn to sheen of ice.

Her face is weather worn and spent,
and her mouth is open, voice sounding,
dialect slipping and sliding down the hill
towards the deepest blue of that cold Atlantic.

And she will go on,
for longer than she thinks,
or can even imagine,
captured in the sepia of film,
and carried in suitcases
across the vast ocean—
to be framed and hung on a wall,
woman not forgotten.

Anchoring

Singsong voices slide upwards
to an open window from painted boats
that unload prawns in Portree's
damp morning light, with shouts of
"Aye, he's yer fella" and bagpipes
blaring from a delivery truck's
hungover scratchy radio.

A boy, scrawny and tall, pulls a
blue boat down a ramp into
the sky-rippled water of this harbour,
dragging its flat bottom on grey pavement,
and then a thunk-swish of water, shifted,
up against the pockmarked cement of pier.

Above, the tall stone church
that hangs on the edge of the bluff
sounds bells, divides the clock-face
of day, while a stray couple walks dockside,
drifting apart and then finding one another
again, hands joining without words,
but with certainty; a mooring.

And then, the sound of kitchen clatter,
from a narrow window high above the road—
a breakfast cleared, a crash of pans,
some eggs, cracked and scrambled,
and the smell of coffee, French pressed,
settling over the salted tang of a nearby sea.

The Standing Stones

At Callanish,
this too pale, ghosted skin
shades itself deep raspberry
in two o'clock sun,
prickling in protest even before
the top of hill is found.

Nearby, that little black dog
with hair in its eyes
stumbles over to me, drunkenly,
offering its neck, tilting its head,
all in the likeness of welcome.

Overlooking Loch Roag,
thirteen tall stones, gneiss-made,
ring-themselves-a-rosie,
around a monolith,
the mother who leads the dance
through nights that spin themselves
with constellations and then rise
again, through centuries, with dawn's sun.

Pre-historic and firmly rooted,
these ancient bones stretch skyward
just as I am drawn to them—
my hand touching, my palm pressed to stone, alive;
my heart, beating, as if for the very first time.

Leaving Waverley

On a fast train south to Newcastle,
trees blur green, feathering
themselves across width of window.
The sea, a muted blue smudge that
stretches lazy off to the east,
hugs the coastline all the way
down to Northumberland—
a Turner painting, or
a suffocating lover.

Fold yourself into the land,
leaving parts buried
in shallow hand dug graves
at the base of Hadrian's Wall,
and then enter the echoic chamber
that is your heart, casting off
the too heavy knit of memory
and reaching, like the desperate
and gathering arms of
too tall windmills,
for some other sky.

Morning Mass at St. Mary's

(for Mum and Dad)

On the banks of the Tyne,
in a town built on the shoulders
of men who mined deepest coal,
I sat in the last row of pews,
eyes turned up to painted heavens
and spotting stray angels' wings, a choir
spinning hymns from the loft above.

Incense and song, rising,
from the deepened red and black
of Victorian tiles underfoot,
to the top of arched rafters—
silver lined dark of high spaces.

And then, down an aisle,
slowed by prayers lifting,
I walked into the stain of glass, etched
against rain-greyed outside skies, watched
the shadow wings of larks loop
across the altar, feather-hopeful.

Later, lighting candles,
incense paled and lights darkened,
I thought of you and crossed myself,
just one more time. Again.

Unsettled, #25
Ireland's Eye, Trinity Bay

(after a photograph by Scott Walden)

Scavengers had been before,
the steeple chain sawed down
so that it lay, sideways,
between the places where
the pews used to live.

In aging afternoon sun,
the last tooth of wall stood,
stubborn against weather and time,
blue sky streaming in through the space
where the window used to be.

The cornerstone was laid in 1927,
last prayers said in 1965,
bookending the place with
those who loved and lost.

Two drownings marked the end,
so townsfolk felt it was time
to go, over sea and then land,
away from the harbour and shore
they had loved for so long.

What's left now?

Strawberries, blueberries, gooseberries,
broken fences, warped clapboard,
weather-worn and tired,
withered facades of homes, left behind,
ghosts slipping into the landscape
as the sun sinks into the sea.

Lost House at Indian Burying Place, Nfld.

(after a photograph by Scott Walden)

The wild grey horse moves through the outport,
racing up the hillside by the cemetery,
avoiding humans, owning the space
left vacant for forty years.

The best preserved house here
has a note pinned to its front door:

Please come in—
but close the door tightly
when you leave.

As if the last family knew
there would be hikers,
or photographers,
or wanderers,
eager to see lives
cast in amber.

Cracked linoleum,
torn floral print curtains,
electric wringer washer,
calendar tilted on the wall,
wood stove and day bed,
all sepia toned echoes
of a life lived near salt water.

Sometimes, in summer,
they come back to fish,
pretending they never even left,
turning backs to shore
hearts to sea.

The Belle of Bell Island

(for Nancy & Maureen)

She was rooted in the earth of island,
found origin in place where sea met sky,
and where men plumbed the depths for iron ore.

Left Bell Island for town,
returning at Christmas,
crossing the iced over tickle,
dodging the heads of seals
on a treacherous journey
over the sculpted waves
of Conception Bay.

A frozen ocean couldn't stop her
from getting home, and then love
took her west to Ontario, even though
Newfoundland still lived in her heart.

The young girl in the photo
waits before a door;
in another image, she
stands near a car, eyes
always off in the distance,
maybe dreaming of
what was, is, or will be.

This is how we leave our marks
on the hearts of daughters who love us;
our stories spoken, over and over,
by voices we loved, given life
even after we've gone.

Dishcloth on Line #1-4 (1997)

(for Mary Pratt)

The woman next door steps out
onto her back porch, pulls in
clothes from her line like a fisherman
draws in catch at end of day.

Not well oiled, line screeches,
protests its purpose. Refuses to comply,
but soon finds itself shifting—moving blankets,
shirts, socks, underwear—back to woman.

Four dishcloths, Pratt woven:
one, to begin, pristine against snow,
while the next catches fire,
sparks rising high into winter sky.
The third is ablaze, furious, proof of life.
Finally, burnt out from the middle,
two strips of linen move in wind,
speak destruction and imply endings.

Over time, fire eats away at things,
just as life frays and wearies; here, aging, erasing,
disappearing the youth that once was,
singes clothespins and hearts
all at once, without care
or backward glance,
leaving field fallow
for next year's planting.

Look, and do not be distracted

(for Mary Pratt)

This gallery is like a church, both
tall spaces that fill with air and
hushed, quiet voices that jar
even when they don't intend to.

On the walls, paintings like
windows into childhood:

Echoes of October's thanksgiving,
with trussed up turkeys, stuffed
and covered with tin foil,
delivered into mouth of
yearning stove in style
of sacrifice or offering.
Gram's tomato aspic salad,
the recipe long lost in
someone's index card frenzy,
wiggling solitary and full of spliced
green olives, making suction noises
when scooped up in serving spoon.
Mum's chicken and dumplings,
chili, turkey soup from bones.

Further on, a riot of paintings,
gathered together in a nest.
Look, and do not be distracted.
Jam jars in bright sunlight, cakes,
half eaten, crumbs on plates and cloth;
fish in sinks, stripped and ready for
the buttered pan, and casserole
all covered and polite in microwave.

Jelly Shelf, 1999

(for Mary Pratt)

*"Still life is the art of the small thing, an art of holding on
to the bits and pieces of our lives."*—Siri Hustvedt

Four jars of jam, sunlight spearing them,
Mason-bound, all. Gather, capture, boil down,
fruit placed in jelly, ambered, as if time
can be stopped, and memory can never betray.

In flashes now, of time spent
before, when you lived on Wembley—
of jam jars laid out on kitchen table,
sterilized by hottest water, gathering
chokecherries from outside bushes
that grew wild in the back yard.

Flowered blouse, roses, Kleenex tucked
into bra or at wrist of green cardigan,
you bustled around that space,
owned it, nested safety when
others most needed it.

Two decades almost gone now;
no one makes jam, but maybe
oatmeal scones with raisins
on rainy days with little
chance of sun or redemption.

A friend sends a cornbread recipe
through email today, conjures time
spent together, feathers slipped under
doors, pieces of sage offered and then
pressed in books. Reminds me of you.

Clear glass of Mason jars, empty now,
gathered on a dusty shelf in fruit cellar,
proof that domesticity has been abandoned
in favour of plane rides abroad, long walks,
poems, wine on the back porch, peace.

Eggs in an Egg Crate (1975)

(for Mary Pratt)

Husks of cracked shells,
placed back in carton,
remnants of whites spilling
over their own halves—
what's lost never to be retrieved.

How many cakes baked,
pancakes mixed, eggs
scrambled or over easy, make up
one woman's life?

Rooted domestic:

An old Chatelaine story,
25 Delicious Ways to Eat Eggs for Dinner,
my grandmother, over hot Kenmore stove,
soft boiling eggs on toast when we felt ill,
and how she raised five kids on Wembley Drive
while her husband prospected up north,
dreams of gold dust in his eyes, while
she made omelettes and kept house.

My mother, blanching beans from
long garden, ready to freeze them for winter,
when the big pot, steaming, foretells
click of furnace turning on, blowing
hot air through vent, drying wet mitts.

Eggs broken, discarded in sink—
conjure Sunday morning breakfast,
old coffee, burnt toast, Dad
dancing on the kitchen floor.

My mother's feet

Since you've been gone,
my feet have lengthened,
shifted into shape of yours.

My hands,
though following your
slender fingers, look
my own, somehow.

Sitting on a step,
glancing down,
I recognize the strong
big toe, angling outwards
as I age, heading towards you.

The Kelly toe, the one
that curves apostrophe
on both feet, is inherited;
memory of family here
and gone.

I have grown into
my mother's feet,
middle-aged, steadfast,
wondering where they
will lead me.

Balancing Acts

I am edge of the world, this world, but lean
into something beyond it.

The photo that hangs on the cupboard door
is pinned there with a small silver nail,
a sepia toned memory in a black frame:
he stands, home on leave, out of uniform,
young, handsome and tall, Black Irish:
she, only two or three, stands upon
the open, flattened plain of his palms, balancing,
her tiny mittened hands bound
in hand knit wool.

Last week, in a summer graveyard,
standing over what's left behind, all ashes now;
fine whiskey poured into a small hole, not for soul.
Fingers tracing surnames etched in granite,
dipping back into western roads on other shores—
touching time, ocean waves, and Ottawa Valley stones,
and then moving northwards to nickel and copper,
a family fashioned by deep rooted mines and slag.

I am edge of the world, this world, but lean
into something other, shimmering
sideways through memory, fingering
edges of old photographs, scalloped,
so that shades overlap,
palimpsest themselves
onto my fair skin.

Solace

(for Cristina)

On a night when empty is what fills me up,
talk of weeping—wild and with abandon—
makes me cringe, curdle and curl up
fetal in a misplaced corner of mind.

Wireless letters flood the screen,
so that I hear her voice in my head:
I think your eyes probably glow when you cry.

There must be solace in that notion,
like a cup of tea on a cold day,
or a shawl to wrap around bent shoulders,
so that tears could redeem themselves—
images from before weighted with mercury
but then, somehow, lined with silver.

I want to believe that my eyes glow,
that sadness will lift:
a bird on an updraft;
a kite summoning itself
into a higher sky,
all painted blue and eggshell;
a heart reaching for another;
a paper snowflake folded
over and over until it
shape shifts into a fan
of pleated memory.

Your eyes
probably glow
when you cry.

And so I look
into a mirror,
find the star hiding
behind these tears,
blink it away.

Orbit

(for Laura)

These stories, of first meetings,
of mingled minds and eyes glancing,
so that your friend said, observantly,

You moved, and then he moved.

Ships passing, then looping around,
drawn together, drifting apart,
and then back again,
ebb and flow,
moved and moving,
so that molecules
shift silently, and are
displaced in heartspace;
an elegant pavan, danced
with hesitant abandon.

He was, your friend said,
a moon caught in your orbit,
circling, advancing, retreating,
and coming close again—
this dance of souls, so delicate,
so new, and yet somehow
even more certain
in its choreography
of serendipity.

You travel on air,
hopes held close to heart,
gathering them in,
wishing, but not,
yearning, but not,
until the pavan is ended,
until the hesitancy is lost,
and palms finally touch
with certainty.

Willa's Poem

Your diaphragm is a jellyfish,
undulating through deep seas
and unmarked spaces.

Too many breaths, broken,
shallow and without substance,
cause hyperventilation.
Soul no longer finds its feet,
goes madly off kilter,
sea legs lost.

Root down.
Press your fingers into the earth.

My hands and feet are branches
of a tree, soft bone and flesh,
clothing the invisible, stripping naked
the pretension and so soul melts,
molting, shedding excess, reaching for more.

I twist from the waist,
fashion a yogic corset,
but then unbind myself,
bloom like a lotus,
up from the muck of muddy land,
resurrecting myself as the jellyfish would,
exploring, undulating, extending, rippling,
returning to older, genetic memory,
only to find myself, anew,
draped in seaweed and coral,
breathing salt water,
evolving.

Incantation Bowl

Come here, Fear:
spiral inwards,
triskele bound,
knotted and looped,
so that you step away
from sharp edges,
the tallest parapet,
the steepest roof,
from the dissonance
of trumpets tuning,
and from the graves
that swallow souls.

And then come here again, Fear,
away from the places where
there are paper cuts to the heart,
away from the cold depths of
a northern lake on
the stormiest of nights,
and from the most broken,
bowl-split and silver lined,
to be mended again in the
newest hour of morning's light.

Spiral inward again, Fear,
like water down an ancient drain,
returning to the lowest point of ground,
levelled, still like a mirror, reflecting,
held in my arms now and dissolving.

Her Hawaii

(for Georgia O'Keefe)

From Sun Prairie, in Wisconsin,
to the badlands of New Mexico,
she searched for wide open spaces,
with deep reverence, as a seeker does.

Flipped through travel brochures,
found one for Hawaii, went there
to paint pineapple posters for Dole,
but fell in love with Maui,
her heart toppled by waterfalls,
lava bridges, bright salted ocean spray.

She was 51 then,
in a marriage that floundered
like a fish out of water,
when she bravely crossed oceans
to find white birds of paradise
and pineapple buds of promise.

Landed on Oahu, stayed in Honolulu,
afterwards shifting to Hana, on Maui;
transfixed by sea caves, sugar cane fields,
tasting tamarind, star fruit, avocado & mango,
so that they soon became colours on canvas,
marked on her heart ever after.

She expected so little of those islands,
after being seduced by the badlands,
but they surprised her, catching her unaware,
sweeping her off her feet, gathering up her heart,
paintbrushes mad with passionate abandon.

Black Lava Bridge, Hana Coast
No. 1, 1939

(for Georgia O'Keefe)

On the edges of things,
away from the pineapple fields,
she found the ocean, smashing itself
against the rough skin of lava
that had naturally found its way to the sea.

Far from the Iao Valley,
where ancient chiefs were buried,
where she painted waterfalls
and rainforest greenery,
this eastern coast of Maui
must have spoken to her with new words.

Here, the lava made a *crazy coast,*
painted all black with bright blue
waves that reflected sky.

At Hana, the waves rise up, *pounding surf
rising* high into the air that hovers,
so that lava poured by Pele is sculpted
into bridges, pathways, gates,
etching out holes where water
sprays, *hissing and blowing,*
letting the light in with each wave's retreat.

She climbed over those rocks,
feeling the push of rough lava
up through the soles of her shoes,
rooting herself as the ocean
rose to meet her with salt water,
ready to paint again.

**The italicized words in this poem are taken from a letter that O'Keefe
wrote to her husband, Alfred Stieglitz, on March 15, 1939.*

He would give it to me

(for Georgia O'Keefe)

She left Stieglitz behind in New York,
descended from the thirtieth floor of
an apartment building where
the view was wonderful,
with towers of steel & glass,
rising up *like tall, thin bottles.*

At Ghost Ranch, north of Santa Fe,
in a tiny adobe house
for more than forty years,
she said,

I feel like myself, and I like it.

The landscape rose up to meet her
as she strode across the barren backs
of rock outcrop, her cotton dress
billowing wildly in desert wind.

The mountain outside her window
haunted her dreams,
waking and sleeping,
so that she felt a new knowing:
God told me, if I painted it often enough,
He would give it to me.

Far from the etched out wind tunnels
of New York's avenues,
she found brightness of soul,
and a sky seen through
the skull of a horse.

In relation to the sky

(for Georgia O'Keefe)

A barrel of bones,
set, forgotten, in the corner,
held by two walls meeting;
they speak to me, curved
and polished.
Either skull or pelvis,
with presence & absence
carved out in shapes,
lenses through which
I can view things.

The sky draws me,
pulls, if only
to unveil land, its
undulations, its hesitations,
stray cows moving through fields
like notes across a music staff,
the collie ushering them on
with demented certainty.

I look hard, see the way the sun
shines and shadows itself, different
in New York than Santa Fe;
same sun, worlds apart,
you shifting from woman to woman
in the way I choose paints,
drawn first to one, then another.

A Very Modern Marriage
(for Alfred Stieglitz)

As mentor, I hung
your works on gallery walls,
sang your praises, spoke your name,
but soon was drawn to
the shape of mouth,
the slope of neck, your eyes,
seductive hands
like sculpture.

I photographed you—
a vast landscape
in one body.

We soon found ourselves,
drifting, ebb and flow,
until you went away,
seduced by heat, adobe,
mountains, the stars
touching your centre
as I couldn't.

You blossomed there,
while I withered, the need
pulsing frantic, desperate
to keep you safe, within,
like a black and white photo,
edges imprisoned by a frame.

Memento Mori: A Poetic Sequence

I) Vanitas

"What you are now, we once were; what we are now, you shall be."
—*a plaque in* Our Lady of the Conception of the Capuchins Church,
Rome.

These shrines tart themselves up,
dress skeletons in bridal gowns
and let wreaths of rosaries
swing from lowered hands—
fingers curled joint by joint,
knuckles crackling,
mannequin arms
and blank faces.

A dog, sitting obediently
at skeletal feet, waits
for a biscuit that will
now never be given—
by an owner who, herself,
sits solitary and draped in shrouds,
next to a neglected stack of vinyl,
Ella Fitzgerald and George Gershwin.

A set of antlers,
bone weary and worn,
sit on blackened bookcase,
next to a spare Buddha—
above a tall tower of books,
gathered for touchstones,
candles all beeswaxed
and melting. Votive and pillars.

II)   The Forgotten Ofrenda

(after Magda Pecsenye's La Muerte de la Memoria)

Your lilies are all white
and gladiolas are not welcome here;
your lover remembers your mind
before it was erased—
chalk laced on a board, cursive and curling,
an artist who painted passion,
indigo blooms on stretched canvas
and lines that ought to have predicted
your spiral into emptiness.

And how you stayed,
mind unravelling like worn wool:
a kite string snagged by wind;
that child's red ball rolling
down a neighbour's hill;
a key dropped down an air vent
not able to be fished out—
until all that remained was
a drawn woman, shrunken and lost,
your hourglass turning in
upon itself, without warning,
sands slipping. Silenced.

Even now, in naked galleries
made bright by Mexican death,
your altar aches, longs for you
to be dressed in jewel tones and
wreathed in marigolds, or hoping
for strings of tangled Christmas lights,
but all that remains, love lost and
mind misplaced, is pale alabaster,
porcelain blooms, a single white taper
that flickers, memory misted.

III) Like Frida (Without Diego)
(after Dia de Muertos es Dia de la Vida)

Majestic, tall and tiny waisted,
she stands, centred and certain,
even though her face is empty—
features taken and not returned.

She looks like Frida,
red blooms crowning her
and a jeweled heart
that sits, collected,
in the centre of a rib cage
that reminds me of birds
and ivory all at the same time.

A rosary swings from her hand,
gathered and salvaged,
each bead a silent prayer
that fingers have rubbed down
now that her god has left her,
abandoned near a city tram station,
preferring industrial murals
to the self-portraiture
of a bedridden artist
who stands next to
a cluster of sugar skulls,
dissolving slowly.

IV)   My Ofrenda

What will I leave, I wonder,
when I go? Behind me, or
before me? Above or below me?

These things, like breadcrumbs
on a woodland trail, soon gathered
by stray birds and wild foxes:

Used up tea bags, Earl Grey;
a rain sodden book of poems,
heart twisted and knotted;
the image of a ship, likely Irish,
all prow heaving and sails flashing,
caught in either sunlight or storm;
a spare dog leash, ready for anything;
eight pens in one bag, its bottom
vast and hard to navigate;
the scent of lavender, for sleep;
birch bark tearing, words written in ink,
tattooed, and not to be left behind;
the feel of old bark on a passing palm,
rubbing up against skin and
tugging at it, seductively;
sweet grass, incensed in hair,
trailing the woods in curls.

Acknowledgements

I am deeply grateful to the poetic friends and mentors who helped me to re-imagine some of these poems over the past few years: Alice Major, Susan Rich, Ken Babstock, John Glenday, Jen Hadfield, Pippa Little, Dawn Kresan, Kathleen Wall, Bernadette Wagner, Kevin Wesaquate, Halli Villegas, and Robert Earl Stewart.

While many of the poems in this collection were written in Northern Ontario, in my hometown of Sudbury, other people and places were important, so I am also especially thankful to: Sue Booth-Forbes of the Anam Cara Writers' and Artists' Retreat in Eyeries, Beara, Co. Cork, Ireland; Philip Adams and the Sage Hill Writing Experience; Heather Clyne and the amazing staff of the Moniack Mhor Creative Writing Centre in Scotland; Grant Munroe of the Woodbridge Farm, as well as Kirk and Elizabeth Munroe, for their kindness and generosity of heart, and for the beauty of the landscape, including the yellow brick house and its spirited views of Lake Erie; and to Denise and David Young, for their quiet retreat space, as well as for the landscape around Bobcaygeon, where the final draft of this manuscript emerged.

Over the years, there have been key people who have helped me to become a better poet and writer. My love and thanks to my mentors and friends: Laurence Steven, Roger Nash, Jack Healy, the late Timothy Findley, Lawrence Hill, and Marnie Woodrow.

I am especially grateful to Gerry Kingsley, for my lovely author photo, and to Trish Stenabaugh, whose artwork graces the cover of this collection.

This little clutch of poems owes its publication to Marty Gervais, who heard me read in Windsor and asked to see my manuscript. Thanks, too, are warmly extended to Alicia Labbé, who took good care of my poems.

Finally, to the small group of close friends who have been with me through dark and light times, steadfast and never giving up when I have gone astray: Jane Rodrigues, my 'second mother;' Brenda Thompson and Jen Geddes, my dear friends; Jenni Hurley, who reads poems with a keen eye to revision; and then, to my most kindred, creative friends, including Trish Stenabaugh, Melanie Marttila, Matthew Heiti, Liisa Kovala, and Sarah Gartshore. I love you people.

About the Author

Kim Fahner lives and writes in Sudbury, Ontario. The first female poet laureate of the City of Greater Sudbury, this is her fourth collection of poems. She has written two plays that have been workshopped at the Sudbury Theatre Centre, and is currently completing her first novel, a historical piece set in a northern mining town outside of Sudbury. Kim is a member of the League of Canadian Poets, the Writers' Union of Canada, and PEN Canada. She blogs at The Republic of Poetry at kimfahner.wordpress.com